1.10

ALFRED

DATE DUE

MAKERS OF CONTEMPORARY THEOLOGY

EDITORS:
The Rev. Professor D. E. NINEHAM
The Rev. E. H. ROBERTSON

PAUL TILLICH, *by J. Heywood Thomas*
RUDOLF BULTMANN, *by Ian Henderson*
DIETRICH BONHOEFFER, *by E. H. Robertson*
TEILHARD DE CHARDIN, *by Bernard Towers*
MARTIN BUBER, *by Ronald Gregor Smith*
GABRIEL MARCEL, *by Sam Keen*
LUDWIG WITTGENSTEIN, *by W. D. Hudson*
MARTIN HEIDEGGER, *by John Macquarrie*
ALFRED NORTH WHITEHEAD, *by Norman Pittenger*
SØREN KIERKEGAARD, *by Robert L. Perkins*

ALFRED NORTH WHITEHEAD

by

NORMAN PITTENGER

JOHN KNOX PRESS

RICHMOND, VIRGINIA

British edition published by the Lutterworth Press
4 Bouverie Street, London, England, 1969

American edition published by John Knox Press
Richmond, Virginia, 1969

Library of Congress Catalog Card Number: 69-14338

Printed in Great Britain

Contents

Preface

This series seeks to introduce the interested reader to 'Makers of Contemporary Theology'—the men whose writing, whether or not intentionally theological or even Christian, has been valuable to modern Christian thinkers in their formulating of the Christian faith. Certainly among philosophers of this century Alfred North Whitehead has been a seminal thinker for one increasingly influential group in the theological world.

In the United States and Canada, there is a large number of Christian theologians who look back to Whitehead with reverence and find his writings an enormous help to them. Recently some of these men have organized a society which meets annually to discuss 'process-thought'. Not all of its members are theologians, and some of them would be hesitant in claiming the name Christian. But all have learned from this Anglo-American thinker, and, although they would disavow the title 'Whiteheadians', they regard him as their intellectual master. In Great Britain, too, interest in 'process-philosophy' has been growing. Not only in Cambridge, where Whitehead himself lived and taught for many years, but elsewhere, theologians are turning to him for help in framing a conceptuality available for Christian use.

As one who is an avowed disciple of this school of thought, I am indebted to the editors and publishers of this series for the opportunity to write a brief exposition for the general reader. This book makes no claim, of course, to being an exhaustive account. It is intended to be suggestive, to provide some background and to give an outline of main emphases (obviously, my own understanding of those emphases!) in Whitehead's thought and in that of his followers in 'process-thinking', for those who wish to continue their study.

I would dedicate this small book to my research-students and others in this University, whose interest in 'process-theology' has been for me both a joy and an inspiration. Only they can understand how much I have learned from discussions with them ; this book is a token of gratitude and affection.

Norman Pittenger.

King's College,
Cambridge.

Introduction

The Concern for Reconception

ALFRED NORTH WHITEHEAD died in Cambridge, Massachusetts, in the United States of America, on December 30, 1947, in his eighty-seventh year. He had lived 'three lives', as he liked to say. The first had been spent in Cambridge, England, where he had been a Fellow of Trinity College and a lecturer in mathematics in the university. The second was in London, where he had taught at London University, serving for a time as President of its Senate. The third, which began in 1924, was at Harvard University, to which he went at the age of sixty-three to become Professor of Philosophy, retiring from active work in 1937 but continuing to live in Cambridge, U.S.A.

His 'third life', in the United States, was the period in which his major philosophical works were written and published. It is these, beginning with his Lowell Lectures, *Science and the Modern World*, in 1925, which have exercised an enormous influence on an increasingly significant movement in Christian theological circles. Whitehead published ten books during those years in the United States, the last of them appearing in the year of his death; it was *Essays in Science and Philosophy*, a collection of various papers and lectures which had not been included in any of his earlier books.

According to his friend Lucien Price, who wrote down a report of conversations with the Whiteheads during the years from 1934 to 1947, the last, or almost the last, remarks of the philosopher (noted by Price as spoken on Armistice Day, November 11, 1947) were these :

> It was a mistake, as the Hebrews tried, to conceive of God as creating the world from the outside, at one go. An all-foreseeing Creator, who could have made the world as we find it now—what could we think of such a

being? Foreseeing everything and yet putting into it all sorts of imperfec-
tions to redeem which it was necessary to send his only son into the world
to suffer torture and hideous death ; outrageous ideas. The Hellenic
religion was a better approach ; the Greeks conceived of creation as going
on everywhere all the time *within* the universe ; and I also think that they
were happier in their conception of supernatural beings impersonating . . .
various forces, some good, others bad ; for both sorts of forces *are* present,
whether we assign personality to them or not. There is a general tendency
in the universe to produce worth-while things, and moments come when
we can work with it and it can work through us. But that tendency in
the universe to produce worth-while things is by no means omnipotent.
Other forces work against it.

God is *in* the world, or nowhere, creating continually in us and around
us. This creative principle is everywhere, in animate and so-called inanimate matter, in the ether, water, earth, human hearts. But this creation is a
continuing process, and 'the process is itself the actuality', since no sooner
do you arrive than you start on a fresh journey. In so far as man partakes
of this creative process does he partake of the divine, of God, and that
participation is his immortality, reducing the question of whether his
individuality survives death of the body to an estate of irrelevancy. His
true destiny as co-creator in the universe is his dignity and his grandeur.[1]

Whether or not Price has given Whitehead's exact words—
we may assume that he has—this quotation provides a good
starting-point for understanding the position which is taken by
contemporary process-thinkers and the Christian theologians
we have mentioned. The key words are in the second paragraph :
'creative principle', 'continuing process' or 'creative process',
'the divine, God', and man's 'true destiny as co-creator'. We
shall see, in the sequel, why Whitehead spoke disparagingly of
'the Hebrews' and their idea of God ; but that he believed firmly
in the reality of 'the divine, God', is beyond question. Nor can
there be any doubt, as we shall also show, that Whitehead
believed that in what he styled 'the brief Galilean vision'[2] there
was a 'revelation in act, of that which Plato divined in theory'—
namely 'a revelation of the nature of God and of his agency in
the world', a disclosure of God not 'as the supreme agency of

[1] *Dialogues of Alfred North Whitehead*, recorded by Lucien Price, 1954, pp.
296–7.
[2] *Process and Reality*, 1929, p. 520.

compulsion' but 'as a persuasive agency'.³ In other words, for Whitehead God is *Love*, both in his nature and in his activity.

The writer of these pages vividly remembers Whitehead's visit to Princeton University in March, 1929, to deliver the Louis Clark Vanuxem Lectures under the title *The Function of Reason* (published the same year). There were three lectures. The first was attended by an audience which entirely filled one of the halls in McCosh, a university building in the centre of the Princeton campus. The third was heard by a mere handful of people, for the difficulty of Whitehead's language was not compensated for by the charm of the lecturer. But it is that charm which I most clearly remember. The rather short, very English, astonishingly youthful-looking lecturer (although he was sixty-eight at the time) ; the benign smile ; the occasional touches of subtle humour ; the capacity to make one feel that here was a man deeply concerned with the truth—all this was most impressive, even when what was being said was extraordinarily difficult to follow. At that time, one felt that here was an eminently good and wise man ; and it is with justice that Price ends his reporting of Whitehead's conversations with the familiar words of Plato about Socrates : '. . . of all the men of his time whom I have known, he was the wisest and justest and best'.

But why is it that this man, more than twenty years after his death, is exerting such an influence on Christian theologians in considerable numbers in North America and now in growing numbers in Britain and elsewhere? I believe the answer is that his philosophical stance, the conceptuality which may be found in or drawn from his works, provides a setting in which the essential Christian faith can be re-thought and re-stated for our own time. Many believe that this approach to things, whatever may be its difficulties in one respect or another, is *appropriate* to that faith in a fashion which is unparalleled in other possible approaches. Hence I conclude this introductory chapter with some remarks on the contemporary concern for Christian re-conception.

³ Quotations from *Adventures of Ideas*, 1933, pp. 170-1.

Matthew Arnold wrote in the last century that men could not do 'without' Christianity, yet they could not do 'with it' as it was then being presented to them. What Arnold said of his own time is equally true for a great number of thoughtful people today. Older ways of formulating the Christian faith, whether these are from Catholic or Protestant sources, seem not to speak meaningfully to such people ; yet somehow they feel that Christian faith itself is or might be meaningful. Especially in recent years, with a growing secularization of culture but with an increasing awareness that human beings require some sense of purpose and direction in existence if their lives are to be more than trivial and inane, there is a yearning for *some* presentation of Christian faith which will be both true to the historical emphases of our Christian tradition and alert to contemporary experience and knowledge.

This explains the ferment in the theological world. Everywhere, among Christian thinkers of all denominations, there is a remarkable stirring ; 'radical theologians' of various sorts are hard at work, seeking ways of making what G. K. Chesterton once called 'the Christian thing' a vivid and compelling reality. Those who are not so 'radical' are equally aware of the situation ; they too are striving to find ways of stating, proclaiming, and thinking through once again the perennial Christian affirmations.

One of the approaches has been through a renewed study of biblical motifs, images, and symbols. What are the enduring 'models' of God and man and their relationship, running through the Old and New Testaments, and how do these present the significance of Jesus Christ? Sometimes these 'models' are thought to have in and of themselves the capacity to communicate meaning to modern man. More often they are 'de-mythologized', re-interpreted in such a fashion that their deepest intention can be accepted as a veridical statement of man's situation, his need for salvation ; and what Christian faith declares provides the answer to that need.

Another way of handling the problem is associated with the attempt to employ the resources of existentialism, with its analysis of man's condition, in such a manner that the faith provides an answer to what that analysis discloses. This is the method of 'correlation', employed by Paul Tillich and others. Or the portrayal of man found in Heidegger may be used as a path to a deeper understanding of 'being', of 'letting be', and of 'new being in Christ'. John Macquarrie has followed this line.

Some theologians, impressed by the difficulty of making metaphysical assertions of any kind (especially in the light of recent philosophical movements which seem to have imposed a 'veto' on metaphysics in anything like the traditional sense), have attempted to present the Christian message in its 'secular meaning', without recourse to the concept of 'God' or 'the divine'. Paul van Buren's recent writing has taken this path. Others do not go quite so far, but with Harvey Cox in his *The Secular City* think that God is to be spoken of only in 'historical' terms, providing the clue to a Christ-like interpretation of man's existence in a world which more and more must be understood in strictly 'secular' ways. And some reject altogether the notion of God, not because they agree with van Buren that the *word* God is meaningless but because (as they put it) 'God is dead'; yet they insist that by taking their stand on Jesus of Nazareth as 'the Man for others', in his contagious freedom and in his outgoing love, they preserve the essence of Christian faith, however profoundly they may depart from what hitherto has been regarded as the necessary theistic ground for that faith.

One realizes that the above paragraphs are so brief as to be a parody of the writers and theologies described. Yet something *like* them is familiar enough in the theological world today. All of them are seriously concerned to make Christian faith a living reality for contemporary people ; all of them must be accorded the respect due to such a serious concern.

But there is another group, the 'process-theologians'. In our final chapter we shall speak of them in greater detail ; here we need only say that Alfred North Whitehead may rightly be called a 'maker of contemporary theology' because of the enormous influence his philosophy has had upon such theologians. Of course, Whitehead is not the only thinker who has worked along these lines. In particular, we must mention the name of his greatest contemporary expounder, Charles Hartshorne. Hartshorne was an assistant of Whitehead's at Harvard; he has developed Whitehead's thought with the use of other sources as well as his own original contributions, which at times are divergent from the doctrines of Whitehead himself.

The Christian theologians who can be grouped together as 'process' thinkers have also been keenly aware of modern existentialism, the biblical work of Bultmann and others, the modern interpretation of history as essentially societal memory, the insight into human nature provided by the depth psychologies as well as by the *Gestalt* and dynamic psychologies, and the contemporary awareness of myth and symbol in man's attempt to grasp the significance of the world and his place within that world. All these have provided material for them in their reconception of the Christian faith. Yet it has been chiefly Whitehead who has influenced them, ultimately if not always immediately. His emphasis on creativity, his seeing of the world as 'creative process', his way of speaking about God in relation to the creation, and his insistence on love (rather than force or coercion, rather even than moral government in the sense of imposed codes or laws) as the key to the structure and dynamic in things—these have been taken by them with the utmost seriousness. Nor is it without significance that the vision of Teilhard de Chardin, who by another path came to much the same conclusions, has spoken directly to them, so that, as Ian Barbour has remarked, Teilhard can also be seen as a 'process theologian'.

But what about Whitehead himself? We shall begin by giving an account of his life and his writing; then we shall consider the chief emphases in his philosophy; and finally we shall speak of the contemporary theological school in which his thought is used in Christian re-conception.

I

Life

Early Years

ALFRED NORTH WHITEHEAD was born in Ramsgate on February 6, 1861. He died in Cambridge, Massachusetts, in the United States, on December 30, 1947, at the ripe age of eighty-six. Between those two dates he had been for many years on the faculty of the University of Cambridge in England, resigning his position as Senior Lecturer in Mathematics in 1910; he had been both a teacher and an administrator at the University of London; and for thirteen years he had been Professor of Philosophy at Harvard University in the United States. The last ten years he had been retired, living in a comfortable flat in Cambridge in the United States and lecturing in many American universities, as well as working on several books which summed up his mature thinking about the world, God, man—and, as a sort of sideline—about 'the aims of education', to use the title of one of his last books.

Despite his long residence in the United States and his (and his wife's) decision to remain there after retirement from Harvard, Whitehead to the end of his days was an Englishman, in accent, in manner, and in attitude. The writer has already mentioned seeing Whitehead at Princeton in the late twenties; on that occasion there could be no doubt of his entirely English personality. Yet he found in the country where he now lived a certain freshness and resiliency which he said he felt was lacking in his own land. However this may be, the fact is that Whitehead's greatest influence as a philosopher was first exerted in the New World; it is only fairly recently that he is being read and his importance as a philosopher recognized in the country of his birth.

Whitehead's father was a clergyman of the Church of England ; his own brother became a famous bishop in the Anglican Church in India. There was a clerical quality in the philosopher which was sometimes amusingly at odds with his incisive and critical remarks about traditional Christian theology. His father had been a schoolmaster in Ramsgate for a number of years before he decided on ordination in 1860. He retained his post as schoolmaster until 1867, when he was made vicar of St Peter's, on the outskirts of Ramsgate.

The boy remained at home until he was fourteen. He was taught by his father, learning from him both Latin and Greek. He imbibed the atmosphere of a clerical home ; and in later years he was accustomed to speak affectionately of his life there. He would mention the way in which he accompanied his father on his parochial visits ; the great influence his father's preaching exerted on him as the older man ('an Old Testament man', he called him) with his great voice, which echoed through the old Norman church which he served, spoke fervently and forcefully to his congregation ; and the delight he felt in knowing one of his father's closest friends, Archbishop Tait. Tait used to drive over to Ramsgate frequently to spend the day ; the young boy even then regarded him as a very great man and once said that 'to have seen Tait was worth shelves of medieval history'.

One of Whitehead's dearest memories was his regular trips to Canterbury itself, only sixteen miles away. He also recalled visits to Richborough Castle, an old Roman fortress in ruins ; and he knew well the place nearby where St Augustine of Canterbury had landed in England in 597, sent by Pope Gregory. He often visited the abbey church at Minster near Ramsgate, the spot where St Augustine first preached the Christian gospel to King Ethelbert of Kent. All this contributed to the development in the boy of the keen historical sense which never left him. It was also during his boyhood that he began that reading of books—books of all kinds, but at this period writers like Dickens, whom he first knew when his grandmother's housemaid read him *Pickwick Papers*—which became his great recreation. As a small child he spent several weeks each spring in London with his grandmother, whose house looked across Green Park. The boy used to see Queen Victoria driving past in her carriage ; he described her as 'a little figure in black, belonging to the unquestioned order of the universe'. All these quotations and recollections of Whitehead come from his charming auto-biographical notes in *Essays in Science and Philosophy*.

When he was fourteen he was sent to Sherborne, the ancient school which he recalled was originally founded by St Aldhelm in Dorset in 741. Whitehead had fond memories of that school, where he was not only a prefect (he recalled caning a disorderly boy, guilty of stealing something or other) but a brilliant student. He continued his Greek and Latin, also doing work in history with a careful study of the Roman and Greek historians. There too he acquired his interest in mathematics, to which he decided to give his life. At the same time he did not neglect reading other books ; at Sherborne he began to love the poets, at that time especially Wordsworth and Shelley, much of whose poetry he knew by heart.

In 1880 he went up to Trinity College, Cambridge. Here he was entirely concerned with mathematics. Yet he said later that thanks to conversations with fellow-undergraduates as well as senior members of the college, above all thanks to his member-ship in 'The Apostles' (the small and always 'anonymous' group who met each Saturday night for free discussion), he became keenly aware of 'politics, religion, philosophy, literature—with a bias toward literature'. Incidentally, he often remarked that it was this 'civilizing self-education' of undergraduates through informal conversation and discussion which was one of the best aspects of the university life in England and he wished there were more of this sort of thing in American education.

Marriage

The year 1885 marked Whitehead's admission as a Fellow of Trinity. Soon he married Evelyn Wade, an Irish girl who had been educated in France and had only come to live in England when she was seventeen. They were a devoted couple, with several children. One son was tragically killed in World War I, a crippling blow for the parents. Their home was at Grantchester, near Cambridge. Whitehead loved the Old Mill House, where they lived, and he spoke frequently of his happiness there—a happiness which was all the greater because from his wife he learned 'that beauty, moral and aesthetic, is the aim of existence'. He confessed that through sharing what he called his wife's 'vivid life' he had experienced an extraordinary deepening and strengthening of his own sensitivity to those areas which mathematics, his own vocation, did not quite provide for.

Writing and Teaching

In 1910 the Whiteheads left Cambridge and moved to London. During his first year in the city, he was engaged in writing ; then, in 1911, he began teaching at University College. Three years later he became a professor at the Imperial College of Science and Technology, also serving the University of London in administrative offices, and towards the end of his time there becoming president of the Senate of the University.

Whitehead was preparing for retirement from active teaching when the invitation came from Harvard University to join its faculty as Professor of Philosophy. This was a great surprise to him. He had already published a number of books ; but they were highly technical, including a *Treatise of Universal Algebra* (1898) ; with Bertrand Russell, the *Principia Mathematica* (1910–13, in three volumes) ; two volumes on *Axioms of Geometry* (1906 and 1907) ; and an *Introduction to Mathematics* (1910). He had also written several books on the philosophy of science, particularly *The Concept of Nature* (1920) which had been delivered as Tarner Lectures at Cambridge. But he had never done anything professionally in general philosophy. The invitation to Harvard had been managed by some American friends, especially

Henry Osborn Taylor, the noted medievalist, who highly
respected Whitehead's quality of mind, and thought that he
would be an admirable addition to the faculty of the great
American university.

In the U.S.A.

Whitehead accepted the invitation. In 1924 he and his wife
crossed the Atlantic and took up residence in Cambridge,
Massachusetts. Before leaving London he had begun to read
deeply in the great philosophical works of the past ; his industry
and his natural interest in the questions which these works posed
made it easy for him to acquire, in a short time, the requisite
technical knowledge. He began his Harvard lectures and
seminars not (as was usual) by offering general survey courses
or by introductory lecturing, but by presenting his own developing ideas.

Those who studied under him tell of his charm of manner, his
sly humour, his profound knowledge, his ability to illuminate
difficult points with telling illustrations of a homely sort ; but
above all they speak of the fascination they felt as their lecturer
or their seminar leader did his own thinking aloud in their
presence and with their help. Whitehead was no dogmatic
lecturer, laying down the law ; he was an inquirer, trying to
discover in company with his students those truths 'of widest
generality' which would provide some understanding of the
world and some answers to the problem about human life in
that world which thoughtful men must inevitably face. Nothing
was cut-and-dried ; all was alive and vital.

One of the points which he made, over and over again, was
that (as he writes in *Adventures of Ideas*, p. 237) 'any doctrine
which refuses to place human experience outside nature, must
find in descriptions of human experience factors which also
enter into the description of less specialized occurrences'. He
was convinced that 'if there be no such factors, then the doctrine
of human experience as a fact within nature is mere bluff, founded

upon vague phrases whose sole merit is a comforting familiarity' (*ibid.*). Here we have already the basic assertion of his fully developed philosophy—that there can be no 'bifurcation' between the scientifically observable and the aesthetically experienced and deeply felt aspects of life. His lectures, so those who heard them tell us, were beautiful examples of this driving desire to find a way of seeing the whole world in its unity, by observation and experiment *and* by feeling and appreciation. And his humility before facts, as well as his compassionate concern for his fellows, could not fail to make its impression on his students.

Lectures and Writings

The year after his arrival in the United States, Whitehead was invited to deliver the Lowell Lectures. He chose for his subject 'Science and the Modern World'; the lectures were published under that title in 1925. Here he presented his considered opinion that the materialistic interpretation given by strictly scientific methodology and experiment is not adequate to the richness of the world as we experience it. There is room for our valuational response and for the religious mode of understanding.

The following year, in four lectures at King's Chapel, Boston, he pursued this last theme. In those lectures, published as *Religion in the Making* (1926), he argued that the fact of religion—arising from man's primitive sense of unfilled void, moving through his feeling of threatening 'enemy' powers on to God known as 'companion'—must find its place in any adequate reading of the way things go. In his own words, 'the present type of order in the world has arisen from an unimaginable past, and it will find its grave in an unimaginable future', but meanwhile 'there remain the inexhaustible realm of abstract forms, and creativity, with its shifting character ever determined afresh by its own creatures, and God, upon whose wisdom all forms of order depend'.[4] He interpreted religion as man's deepest vision of reality; and he contrasted Buddhism, which he described as

---

[4] *Religion in the Making*, 1926, p. 154.

'a metaphysic generating a religion', with Christianity which is 'a
religion seeking a metaphysic'.[5] What 'is primary' in Christianity
is 'the religious fact'. 'The Buddha gave his doctrine to enlighten
the world', he said. 'Christ gave his life. It is for Christians to
discern the doctrine'.[6]

Lectures delivered at the University of Virginia dealt with
man's symbolizing powers and their significance; these were
published in 1927 as *Symbolism: Its Meaning and Effect*. The
lectures were remarkable for their grasp, long before our own
day, of the problems raised by man's linguistic efforts to express
meaning. The final words are very telling, with their theological
overtones:

> The art of free society consists first in the maintenance of the symbolic
> code; and secondly in fearlessness of revision, to secure that the code
> serves those purposes which satisfy an enlightened reason. Those societies
> which cannot combine reverence to their symbols with freedom of
> revision, must ultimately decay either from anarchy, or from the slow
> atrophy of a life stifled by useless shadows.[7]

The amount of work which Whitehead did in those years is
remarkable. In 1928 he collected lectures and papers on education which he published under the title *The Aims of Education*.
The following year, 1929, his greatest book made its appearance:
the Gifford lectures, delivered at the University of Edinburgh
during a return visit to Britain in 1927–28. Entitled *Process and
Reality*, this is an extremely tightly packed and very difficult
volume. To understand it requires not only historical awareness
and scientific knowledge but the closest attention to its termin-
ology, since Whitehead felt obliged to create a new language in
order to express his deep sense of the processive nature of reality,
including deity. What is more, the book contains in its first edition
and in all subsequent ones a multitude of typographical errors,
while it is also rather disorderly in its development of his
'doctrine'. Happily, Professor Donald Sherburne of Vanderbilt
University in the United States has produced a carefully arranged

[5] *Ibid.*, p. 50.
[6] *Ibid.*, p. 55.
[7] *Symbolism: Its Meaning and Effect*, 1927, p. 88.

'Key to Whitehead's Process and Reality' (published under that
title in 1966) which provides for the careful reader an orderly
statement of Whitehead's ideas, with notes that explain new
terms and with an excellent summary of each of the main points.

The Vanuxem Lectures at Princeton, *The Function of Reason*,
to which I referred in the first chapter, also appeared in 1929.
Their title indicates the topic discussed. Four years later, in
1933, *Adventures of Ideas* was published. This volume is in four
parts : the first deals with sociological matters, approached from
a 'process' position ; the second is cosmological, discussing the
world and its regularities as well as the novelties which appear
within it, and including a chapter (to which we shall later make
special reference) on 'The New Reformation', in which the
author discusses Christian faith and theology ; the third is
philosophical, devoted to a further discussion of ideas found in
Process and Reality ; and the fourth, a remarkably beautiful section, has to do with 'civilization', the societal pattern of man's
life in an evolutionary cosmos, with chapters on truth, beauty,
the relation of these two, adventure or zest as characteristic of
man as he shares in the onward thrust of the creative process,
and peace or the establishment of enduring harmony in which
'the dreams of youth and the harvest of tragedy' bring forth 'the
union of Zest with Peace—that the suffering attains its end in a
Harmony of Harmonies'—God himself (pp. 294–5).

A small volume called *Nature and Life* includes lectures given
at the University of Chicago in 1933–34 ; it was published in the
latter year. These lectures were later included in a larger book
entitled *Modes of Thought*, which also contains lectures given at
Wellesley College in 1937–38, after Whitehead's retirement from
Harvard, and an address to students at Harvard and Radcliffe
(the women's college associated with Harvard). In many ways
this is Whitehead's simplest and most attractive publication ; it
appeared in 1938. Finally, as he entered the last year of his life,
nearly ten years later, he authorized a collection of his essays and
lectures during the intervening period which was published in
1947 ; the title is *Essays in Science and Philosophy*.

Process-Thought

'Nature and Life' and the other lectures in *Modes of Thought* perhaps provide as good an introduction to his final and settled views as any of his books. These Chicago lectures might well be read first by any who wish to understand 'process-thought'; then one could read the opening sections of *Science and the Modern World*, followed by *Adventures of Ideas*, *Religion in the Making*, and *Symbolism*, coming at last to the Gifford Lectures.

In 1954, Lucien Price gave the world his records of Whitehead's conversations over many years. *Dialogues of Alfred North Whitehead* is a charming book; to read it is to get the 'flavour' of the man who is talking informally and 'off the cuff', telling his memories of days long past, giving his opinion on current affairs, intimately portraying his own inner life. But it is a dangerous book, since readers may feel that in it they are getting White-head's *considered* views, whereas in fact they are hearing only his occasional conversation when he was in a relaxed mood. It is especially dangerous when it is taken as providing the context for the ideas advanced in his carefully written books. *Dialogues* should be read the other way on; it is only when one has mastered the Whiteheadian philosophy in its broad outlines that one can see how, and why, the incidental comments reported by Price were made—and could be made. None the less, all lovers of Whitehead and all who respect him as a philosopher must be grateful to Price for keeping the records and for letting us have them in all their spontaneity and freshness.

Final Years

Whitehead's last years were spent in something of the peace of which he spoke in the final section of *Adventures*. The 'zest' was there, but so also was the 'tragic beauty'. He was saddened by the Second World War, he suffered with his beloved native land in its ordeal, he missed old friends who had died before him.

Yet there was 'harmony', for he remained serene in the midst of the world's turmoil, not by denying or minimizing the conflict but by seeing through it and in it the working out of the purposes of good which (as he was deeply convinced) are basic to the creative process. One could say that he did himself 'partake of this creative process' (as he put it) and thus found 'his dignity and grandeur'. He died full of years and much beloved by all who knew him ; only now is his influence beginning to be felt to the degree which some of us think it merits.

Note on Charles Hartshorne

We have said earlier that Professor Hartshorne is the outstanding living exponent of Whitehead's vision, although he has developed his philosophy on his own lines. His writing is clear, eminently readable, and deeply Christian. A note about this American philosopher is appropriate in concluding this chapter about Whitehead's life and writings.

Like Whitehead, Charles Hartshorne is the son of an Anglican divine ; his father was for many years rector of a parish of the Episcopal Church near the city of Philadelphia in Pennsylvania. Hartshorne was born in 1897. He attended Haverford College, but with the outbreak of World War I he went to France to serve as an orderly in an army hospital. He completed his university work at Harvard, where he also received his doctorate in philosophy. From 1923 to 1925 he studied in Germany at Marburg and Freiburg, returning to Harvard as an instructor in philosophy and as an assistant to Whitehead. As a research fellow at Harvard, he began (with Paul Weiss) the editing and publication of the collected papers of the little-known philosopher Charles Sanders Peirce, a task that continued for many years afterward.

In 1928, Hartshorne was called to the University of Chicago where he spent twenty-seven years, not only teaching philosophy in the University itself but also assisting in teaching in the Divinity School attached to the University. During those years he lectured extensively, visiting among other places the Goethe University in Frankfurt, Germany, and Melbourne University in Australia. He joined the philosophy faculty of Emory University in Atlanta, Georgia, in 1955 ; three years later he lectured at Kyoto University in Japan as a visiting professor, also serving for a time as a visiting professor at the University of Washington in the Far West of the United States. Finally in 1962 he went to teach at the University of Texas, in Austin ; the following year he was appointed to the Ashbel Smith Professorship of Philosophy there. Since then he has again visited several Asian countries to lecture on philosophy. In 1967 he lectured at universities in Great Britain, including London, Cambridge, Manchester, Glasgow and Edinburgh.

In the books which have come from his pen he has untiringly expounded and defended what he calls 'neo-classical theism'. The first of these works, apart from a study of 'sensation' considered psychologically and philosophically, was entitled *Beyond Humanism* (1937). With its successor, *Man's Vision of God* (1941), it argued that there is a third possibility between the view which sees God as wholly absolute (hence entirely un-related) and that which sees in the world nothing but contingency (hence the denial of *any* theism). This third possibility is a conception of God as in certain 'abstract' respects absolute (*eternally* faithful, *always* loving, *unfailingly* related to his creatures) and in certain and more 'concrete' respects relative or relational (in the actuality of his loving, caring, creative action, etc.).

Following these early works, Hartshorne has developed along Whiteheadian lines a view of the world as 'social process', in which God is the supremely relative (related) creative and dynamic principle, personal in nature, necessary—hence Hartshorne's great interest in Anselm's ontological argument, about which he has written two large books—and inescapable, even if not always recognized as God. He has differed from Whitehead in respect to the necessity for 'eternal objects', in his more 'psychic' portrayal of the *telos* in each level of integrated creation, and in his insistence that God must be conceived as a 'process' of such a sort that his genuine personality is asserted. Into his thought have entered ideas derived from his Harvard teacher, William Ernest Hocking, as well as from Peirce's argument for 'chance', albeit a 'controlled chance' (since the universal movement cannot get out of hand, thanks to the persuasive governance of God as Love), which characterizes creation. He has emphasized his conviction, present also in Whitehead, that radical freedom is found in the created order.

Finally, Hartshorne is interested in the religious implications of 'process-philosophy'. His most recent book, *A Natural Theology for our Times* (1967), spells this out ; and in lectures and essays which will be collected and published within the next year or so, it is made even clearer. His specifically *Christian* use of the 'neo-classical' position, coupled with his keen awareness of the presence of religion among all kinds of men, has made his development of 'process-thought' singularly attractive to such theologians as Schubert Ogden and L. C. Birch, who have employed it to good effect in their thinking about God's mode of relationship to the world, his 'act' in history, and the nature of the person of Christ.

Hartshorne feels that 'classical theism', especially as represented in the scholastic tradition in Catholicism (he often mentions the name of Thomas Aquinas), has consistently emphasized only one possible interpretation of 'perfection' as applied to God. This is the notion that to be 'perfect' *must* mean to be absolute, self-contained, self-sufficient, un-affected. But that is to take as our model for God a 'perfection' which we find reprehensible when we observe it in one of our fellow-men. There is another notion of 'perfection', one which we admire when we see it embodied in another man : to be perfect can mean to be 'unsurpassable by any other, yet to be surpassable by oneself', to be open and loving with *all* others (not just with a few), to be entirely consistent and faithful in all one's relationships so that one can always be counted on, trusted, and loved by others.

It is Hartshorne's conviction that only this latter notion of 'perfect' may properly be used in speaking of God. He is perfect in love, in goodness, and in knowledge of the past and present and of all relevant possibilities in the future, but without dictating or controlling the creatures or 'knowing' the creature's choice before they are made, since theirs is genuine freedom. Yet because he is 'perfect' in love and inexhaustible in his goodness, he may be trusted completely ; he will always bring the best out of any and every circumstance, although that victory must for him (as for us) be at the cost of pain. Hence, the compassionate love and self-identification of God with men shown in Jesus Christ is the best symbol for deity, as the Cross (where triumph was achieved through suffering) symbolizes God's manner of working in his world. In Wesley's phrase, God is 'pure unbounded love'.

In these and other ways, Hartshorne suggests re-interpreting the basic affirmations of Christian faith. One point is of special interest : God in his 'consequent nature' (Whitehead's language is used here) unfailingly 'remembers' all that has taken place in the actual occasions in the creation ; nothing which is of real value is ever lost. All that can be 'saved' is saved and used by God on future occasions to bring about, through his persuasive action, widely-shared good. This is true even if, as Hartshorne thinks, we need not posit our own continued conscious existence after death. *God* knows the good and he uses it for greater good, as he uses also evil, once overcome, for greater good. So in the last resort, for Hartshorne, Mother Julian's vision is sheer truth : 'All shall be well, all shall be well, all manner of thing shall be well'. *God is Love* and his glory is precisely his activity in loving.

2

Thought

Process-Thought and its Emphases

CENTRAL to process-philosophy as Whitehead developed it, is the conviction that we must look at experience *as a whole*. We must also look at the world in the same way, taking account of all the data which are presented to us and refusing to reject or disregard any aspects which do not fit in with some pre-conceived notion of what the world is like. Hence we may say that unity of experience and the unity of the world in which that experience is enjoyed must be primary in our effort to understand the way in which the world goes and the meaning of our experience in the world.

Whitehead had specialized in mathematics. He was also an expert in the field usually known as mathematical physics and its associated disciplines. At the same time, as we have seen, he was sensitive to literature, especially to poetry. He had a keen 'aesthetic' awareness, in the broad sense which he himself insisted on giving that adjective : that is, the whole range of 'felt' life. He knew about 'religious experience' from within, since he had been brought up in a strongly religious home and knew with certainty that, no matter how he might differ in conceptual matters from his father and from others who were in the professional sense (as we might put it) engaged in the activities of established religious groups, the convictions which they held were not based on fancy or wish-fulfilment but on deep realities in their own lives. Thus, Whitehead himself represented a reconciliation of what Lord Snow in recent years has described as 'the two cultures'. He was both a scientist and a humanist, and he respected both aspects of human experience. He was sure that both the precise experimental and observational work of the scientist and the appreciative, valuational interests of the poet, the artist, the musician, and the man who feels deeply some sense of comradeship or communion with a reality not observable by scientific instruments nor reached by the use of scientific methods, must be taken seriously into account in any portrayal of the world and of man which presumes to claim to be adequate to the given material.

In particular, as a quotation in the last chapter has shown, Whitehead believed that *human* experience, in all its richness and variety, is part of nature ; we cannot cut man and his experience off from the natural order, as if that experience could contribute nothing to our grasp of what nature is like and what is going on there. For him it was the failure of much of the science of the nineteenth century, with which he was so familiar, that it had thought it possible to make precisely that disjunction. The result of such an attitude, he was convinced, was a picture of the world which was 'a bluff' or, as he said in another connection, 'a fake'. Here biological study, and more particularly the evolutionary science which demonstrated man's emergence from a sub-human animal species, has made its invaluable contribution ; it had made inescapably clear to all who attended to it that man is 'organic' with nature. If man cannot be understood unless his animal ancestry is taken into account, neither can the world in which he emerged be understood unless man (as a part of nature, tied in with it and intimately at one with it, despite all his difference from it and despite the unique quality of his existence as a conscious and purposive emergent) is regarded with equal seriousness. And this meant that the richness and variety of human experience, above all in its 'felt' aspects, provide us with data that must be used by the philosopher.

Since he saw man and the world in this way, Whitehead claimed that there were three main points which must be stressed. First, there was an element of 'enjoyment' in experience. Certainly this was obvious at the human level ; it was also capable of being 'generalized', as he liked to put it, so that something analogous could be predicated at other levels as well. The world, then, is characterized by such a sense of satisfaction or fulfilment as is discovered, at its most intensive, in human experience.

But secondly, that 'enjoyment' is not given ready-made; it is achieved. In other words, throughout the world of nature as well as in human life there is 'aim'. This is found in differing degrees of intensity and with varying degrees of consciously-known and intentionally-directed striving; yet it is a serious failure to take into account all the facts if supposedly hard-headed thinkers refuse to see that such 'aim' towards 'enjoyment' in man must be indicative of 'aim' throughout the cosmos.

In the third place, there is 'creativity'. By this Whitehead intended the reality of possibility or potentiality, and the capacity to realize these, with the 'advance' which made that realization possible—and this not only in human experience but more generally in the world as a whole. We are confronted by, and we are participant in, a dynamic *process*, in which the occurrences which compose the world are getting somewhere, whatever that 'somewhere' may be. Very simply, there is a 'going-on' in the world, from potentiality to actualization; and this is a dynamic and vital movement. We have to do with no mere shuffling of a pack of cards, no mere re-arranging of hard and intractable atoms; on the contrary, we have to do with an epigenetic move-ment, in which novelty makes its appearance. Whitehead might have made his own the lovely phrase of G. M. Hopkins, 'There lives the dearest freshness deep down things'. And out of that 'freshness', or realm of creative possibility, appear the novelties which give both the world and our experience an equal 'fresh-ness'.

There is a 'perishing of occasions', as the old reaches its ful-filment and in its particular configuration 'passes away'; but at the same time there is the new, built out of the old, which thus serves in providing material upon which something genuinely novel can be woven. Abiding value, the genuine contribution made by that which perishes, can never be lost; it is taken up into, used by, and made contributory to, that which continues in all its wonderful freshness with its capacity for furthering 'creative advance'.

In our attempt to grasp what experience so interpreted and the world thus envisaged has to tell us, Whitehead demanded that the philosopher must be open to *all* which comes to him from every area. Above all, he believed that 'living emotion', of which the philosopher F. H. Bradley had written, must be given a central place. 'The basis of experience', said Whitehead, 'is emotional. Stated more generally, the basic fact is the rise of an effective tone originating from things whose relevance is given'.[8] Such awareness suggests that we both *grasp and are grasped by* (Whitehead's technical word here is 'prehend') this or that moment of experience—and the same must be true through-out the cosmos, in respect to every occasion or occurrence or event (Whitehead generally used the term 'actual entity'). To deny this would be to cut human experience off from nature and to fail to recognize the genuinely revelational quality of that experience.

Because the world is a society of mutually 'prehending' occasions, Whitehead felt that a useful word for describing it was 'organismic'. It is made up of organically inter-related and organically developing entities—not of static substances or entirely discrete (separate and separable) bits of matter in motion.

Presuppositions and Methodology

In the exposition which follows, we shall not employ—save where it is absolutely necessary—technical Whiteheadian terms. Whitehead's language, however, is not anything like so difficult as many have thought. Much of it is derived from a variety of sources, including Hume, Bradley, William James, and other philosophers, as well as from scientific sources and literature. His thinking is closely related to these and other well-known thinkers who preceded him in the construction of philosophical

[8] *Adventure of Ideas*, p. 226.

schemes or systems. Since we do not use his technical terms, we shall not attempt to set forth a neatly systematic development of Whitehead's thought either. For our purpose—which is to show those aspects of Whitehead's philosophy which have a special appeal to Christian theologians—it is much more convenient to provide a general presentation of what he himself would have called his 'vision of reality'. But before we do this, a few words must be said about the Whiteheadian presuppositions and methodology.

In respect to the former, perhaps enough has been said in the preceding section. Yet we should add a few additional remarks. First, let us note that Whitehead once said this : 'Philosophy asks the simple question, What is it all about?'[9] That is to say, he believed that when a man engages in philosophy he must necessarily concern himself with the attempt (however perilous) to find ultimate meaning—'what is it *all* about?' (italics mine). He can write[10] the following important sentences :

> Philosophy is not a mere collection of noble sentiments ... It is not— or, at least, it should not be—a ferocious debate between irritable philosophers. It is a survey of possibilities and their comparison with actualities. In philosophy, the fact, the theory, the alternatives, and the ideal, are weighed together. Its gifts are insight and foresight, and a sense of the worth of life, in short that sense of importance which nerves all civilized effort.

Thus he says[11] that philosophy, as he sees it, 'is the endeavour to frame a coherent, logical, necessary system of general ideas in terms of which every element of our experience can be interpreted'. Each of the adjectives here used should be noted carefully : *coherent, logical* relationship, and *necessary* induction from experience. This interpretation includes what earlier in the same book[12] he has named 'natural science' and the concepts to which it gives rise, *and also* 'the aesthetic, moral, and religious interests' of men, out of the totality of which the philosopher

---

[9] Quoted in *The Philosophical Review*, Vol. XLVI, 1937, p. 178.
[10] *Adventures of Ideas*, p. 125.
[11] *Process and Reality*, p. 4.
[12] *Ibid.*, p. vi.

seeks 'to construct a system of ideas'. But Whitehead does not
claim that any such system, certainly not his own, is final ; as he
remarks, 'the besetting sin of philosophers is that, being merely
men, they endeavour to survey the universe from the standpoint
of gods'. Granted the absurdity of such a stance, he yet believes
that it is entirely legitimate and proper for a thoughtful man to
think about and endeavour to work out a 'system of ideas'
which fulfils the conditions noted above.

Doubtless there will be a variety of such proposed 'systems'.
Every effort should be made to achieve a reconciliation between
or among them ; surely each of them contains some glimpse of
the truth. This also suggests that any given system, such as his
own, is open to criticism, correction, and development ; and the
invitation implied in Whitehead's own writing explains why no
'Whiteheadian', no process-thinker, agrees in all details with
others who take the same general position. We are not dealing
here with a cut-and-dried metaphysic ; on the contrary, process-
philosophy in following Whitehead welcomes various applica-
tions, differing ways of stating implication, and open-ness to
other approaches drawn from other 'visions of reality'.

When we come to Whitehead's methodology, we may sum
up his procedure by noting that it is both *rational* and *empirical*.
Or perhaps the order of words should be reversed. It is *empirical*,
in that it begins from the most careful study of some given,
perhaps quite restricted, area. This may be science in any of its
branches ; it may be religious experience or moral awareness or
the realm of the 'aesthetic'. But it is also *rational*, for from these
careful studies of particular areas, generalizations are made.
And the tests for such generalizations are the coherence, logical
implication, and necessity of what is being affirmed. Furthermore, every generalization must be tested constantly by a reference back to the empirical evidence as this has been observed or
studied or experienced in the several different fields or areas of
interest.

How is the study or observation to be carried out? At this
point, Whitehead dwells on the importance of intuition, which

for him is a profound awareness, deeply felt, of the particular datum under consideration. But intuition is of various sorts ; it may be 'sensuous' or 'non-sensuous', and it may be directed towards the type of awareness which is more 'mathematical' in quality. And intuition may operate in different realms. The moral sense of the rightness of things is one example, another is the artist's empathetic awareness, and still another the religious perception that through and in our stream of experience and the changing world there is a persisting goodness or love, not static in nature but more than *mere* successiveness.

With this methodology of empirical investigation and rationally ordered generalization, Whitehead proceeds to look at the world. As we have seen, he is not content with one area of experience ; to concentrate entirely on any one field of interest would be to impoverish one's grasp of the totality of things 'as they go on', while it would also diminish the validity of the generalization which is to be made. One must seek to include as much of experience, and as many varieties of experience, as one can manage to grasp. It is this which leads him to what we have already called his organic (or societal) vision of the cosmic process. There is a 'wholeness' about his vision which has often been lacking in philosophical systems which restricted their attention to fewer fields or which were content to make great generalizations from the special enquiries which happened to be attractive to their authors.

This insistence on what we have styled 'wholeness' also explains Whitehead's interest—one might even say, delight—in such inter-disciplinary research as (for example) bio-chemistry and other types of study in which more than one line of inquiry is seen as relevant to understanding entities of a 'molecular' sort. He wanted scientists and artists, saints and scholars, thinkers of every type, to pool their resources and to share their researches. Only in this way could men ever hope to see more deeply into the meaning of the various dynamic processes and into the abiding structures in terms of which those processes may be more or less adequately described.

c

A final word should be said about the question of language itself. For Whitehead language is symbolization, through which some rationalizing of man's perceptions and hence some rational ordering of his concepts takes place. It is always, and also, one of man's agencies in understanding that which he perceives and about which he makes conceptual statements. But verification is found, not merely in the right and appropriate *use* of language —which inevitably, because it is symbolic, includes apprehensions deeper than the bare rationality involved—but also in the continual reference back to the particular observations of what in fact is experienced and hence spoken about. Strictly scientific (mathematical, experimental) verification could not be enough ; the whole range of experience, in all its 'feltness', must be taken very seriously into account.

The Cosmic Process and its Description

'The contrast real-unreal has nothing particularly to do with the contrast being-becoming'. So wrote Professor Hartshorne in an essay published in 1968.[13] That sentence, appearing in a brief study of the possibility of using 'process-philosophy' as a conceptuality for theology, puts briefly but exactly the main stress in Whitehead's description—if that is the right word— of the cosmic process. It has been an error, found in most if not all philosophers, to think that 'being' is more *real* than 'becoming' ; hence that a world, or anything else, in process must be less real than a world, or anything else, which may be spoken of in terms of *stasis* or self-contained and unchanging being.

But here already we have the illicit confusion to which Hartshorne referred. 'Real' versus 'unreal' can and should mean 'true' versus 'false or fictitious' or (as Hartshorne himself noted) 'merely feigned or falsely believed'. It has nothing to do with the question of whether or not being or becoming shall be more *basic* (not more *real*) in the world or in anything else.

[13] *Philosophical Resources for Christian Thought*, p. 44.

Whitehead was convinced that proper interpretation of experience and the result of correct observation of the world will show that *process* is absolutely basic. In other words, becoming is the more concrete 'reality' (always remembering the proper use of that term), while being is an abstraction from the concrete facts which we know, experience, and are. This is the cornerstone of the whole enterprise of 'process-thought'. It regards the persisting centring of attention on being as basic as nothing less than an idol which is worshipped servilely but thoughtlessly by very intelligent and very good men who should have known better and who often enough, in the course of their philosophizing or theologizing, *did* know better but were unable to escape the power of the idol which dominated their thinking. When it speaks of God, process-thought regards as equally misleading the stress on 'self-contained and self-centred being' in the sense of *ens realissimum* (most real being) or *esse a se subsistens* (being subsisting from itself), terms commonly used to signify utter *aseity* as God's 'root-attribute'.

This may seem an extraordinary assertion, but consideration of the cosmic process as we encounter it, live in it, and ourselves are part of it, will give support to what Whitehead and his disciples have said on the matter. Let us now attempt to sketch out the way that process does manifest itself to us.

Five comments may be made.

First, we have to recognize that ours is most certainly a processive world—or, if one prefers, a world of evolutionary change. Today it is common knowledge that we do not live in what might be styled a 'fixed order'; things are on the move. From the lowest level of energy up to man himself, what we see is change. This does *not* mean that there are no fairly settled patterns which may be discerned in the movement or process of change ; neither does it suggest that there are no identifiable 'routings' of the entities of which the world is made up. It *does* mean that things do not 'continue in one stay'. If we wish to describe what is going on at any level in the whole creative order, we must do so by talking of where things are getting, what they are doing, how they are realizing whatever potentialities they may have been given. In other words, what we see and know is 'how things *are getting on*' rather than 'what things *are*'. None the less, it *is* an 'order', in which there are limits set for actualization of potentialities, in which certain possibilities are realized rather than other conceivable possibilities, and in which there is (as we shall see in a moment) a certain direction or aim.

There is no mere unfolding of what has always been the case, either ; what evolutionary science, with its application in appropriate ways to the many non-biological levels, portrays for us is much better described in the phrases used by A. S. Pringle-Pattison many years ago : 'continuity of process with the emergence of genuine novelty'. New things happen ; but they happen with linkages with what went before, with astoundingly intricate relationships with what goes on contemporaneously, and with enormous consequences for what is to happen or what may happen in the future.

This is a world in which time is very real. It 'takes time' for things to 'come to be'. Becoming is temporal, not static or instantaneous. It takes time, too, for the results to be shown for what they are, with the consequences as they occur, and with the modifications that they introduce into the various patterns with their limits of possibility. Further, there appears to be an element of 'chance' in the world ; yet it is not *just* chance, as if 'any old thing could happen'. There is a 'getting-somewhere'. There is a direction or aim, not only at the level of consciousness (of the sort *we* know) but at the level of living-matter ; and even below that, if what some of our most acute modern scientists say is correct, there is direction or aim in the inanimate and physical world too. This is no Paleyan teleology, after the analogy of the watchmaker and his watch. It has more to do with what in the United States is called 'the big picture' than with the arrangement of the specific details—it is more molecular, one might say, than it is atomic. One thinks here of the work done by Sir Alister Hardy and reported in his recent Gifford Lectures, or of the writings of Dr W. H. Thorpe in the general biological field, while in the physical sciences, the discussion by Dr Ian Barbour in his *Issues in Science and Religion* is to the point. The purposive quality in the world makes it proper to speak not of a machine grinding along without aim but of a process which in organic instances of occurrence, occasion, and event is moving towards goals that are realized by appropriate decisions and in greater or less degree at every level.

But since this is the case, the second point is that the world is a dynamic enterprise. To talk about 'substances' (as static or inert entities) is a misrepresentation of the known facts. We are in error when we attempt to freeze a living process of becoming into a connected series of things. What we know are occasions or 'actual entities' and what we have called 'routings of occasions', whose nature is to 'become' what they have it 'in them' to become, functioning in this or that way as they realize (or by decision refuse to realize) their potentiality.

Man, for example, is not a thing which may be described in static terms as *this* or *that* completed entity; he cannot be talked about morphologically, so far as philosophical understanding is concerned, as if he were a specimen on a dissecting-table. He is a dynamic process. To *be* a man (in the only viable sense of that verb) is to 'become man', to be on the way to the actualization of the specific potentialities which are given at the human level. Some of the definitions of man which have been fashionable in traditional philosophy have in effect spoken about him as if he were only a 'specimen', open to dissection. Even in the biological realm, we 'murder to dissect'; a cat when it is being dissected is not a live cat, it is a *dead* one. Much valuable information may be gained by the dissecting operation; but it is not information about the living, scratching, purring animal. It is the dynamic quality of the living cat which essentially constitutes its 'catness', if one may put it so.

A good deal of metaphysical talk has been vitiated by a hankering after 'essences', in an effort to define man without regard to his dynamic quality. But the same is true of much talk about what is given throughout the process. In consequence,

we have been the victim of a distorted picture of what the world
is really like.

Thirdly, we are confronted by, we live in, and we are part of a
societal or organismic world. Things affect one another, at
every level ; everything lives in and with and for every other
thing, however remote and infinitesimal the connections may
seem to be. There is mutual prehension, as Whitehead puts it.
The creation is a series of occasions in which each entity is pene-
trated by and penetrates the others, and in which all are in inter-
relationship with each other. No man, no thing, is 'an island
entire unto itself' ; every man, every thing, is tied together in a
'bundle of life'. Drop a pencil on the floor and the whole of
'reality' is different from that moment ; for that simple act has
repercussions and results throughout the succeeding process.
There is mutuality, give-and-take, wherever we turn. Hence
we ought not to think of discrete entities, in the sense of self-
contained and insulated particles ; we should see an open-ness,
a 'being affected by' as well as an 'affecting' which is characteristic of the process in its every event.

But in the fourth place, no occurrence or occasion is identical
with any other ; nor are they all on the same level of significance.
In the ongoing movement there are particular moments which
(in a word of Whitehead's) are 'important'. This concept is of
the highest significance for our understanding of how the world
goes. A given moment of experience, a given configuration of
occasions, a particularly vivid *this* or *that* (whatever it may be)
can illuminate what has gone on before its appearance or emergence ; can enter into peculiarly intimate relationships with what
surrounds it and with which it has its connections, influencing
and being influenced by those occasions ; and can open the way
for novel, perhaps surprising, developments in the future.
Usually what is 'important' is taken to be such because of its
'aesthetic' quality—the feelings which it evokes and which in
some way seem to participate in that which evokes them. As
we have said earlier, by 'aesthetic' is not meant artistic creations
alone (although such may be in the picture, from time to time).

The word points to the deep feelings which the particular occasion awakens ; our very language shows this, for we say that this or that 'appeals to us', 'attracts us', 'lures us', 'strikes us', 'makes its impact upon us'. The important whatever-it-is is *there*, since it is not a matter of fanciful dreaming ; yet it is not there alone, for it possesses (although this is not quite the right word) the capacity to awaken the response which impels us to say, 'Yes, that's it!'

That which is thus 'important' provides us with a clue or key to our interpretation of ever wider fields in the process. For Whitehead, certainly, human experience in all of its richness and variety, known to us in so many ways, was very important in his reading of the world and its dynamic structured process. What is more, this or that particular moment in human experience may have for us a singular importance in the same kind of way. Perhaps it is along such lines that one may speak of some one compelling historical personality (the Christian would speak of Jesus) as making available a clue to the basic 'going-on' which refers ultimately to God himself. But of this more will be said in our last chapter.

Finally, Whitehead speaks frequently and insistently of 'tenderness' and 'persuasion', words which for him denote love. This persuasiveness is for him much more significant in the final analysis than the coercion which on the surface seems so obvious in the world. It is by the patient, often slow, yet enormously effective influence of 'lure' and 'appeal', of tenderness and love-in-action, that most is accomplished in the world. Real omnipotence is not found in the exercise of control by force but in what Aristotle once called 'the power of the beloved over the lover'. There is, said G. M. Hopkins in the phrase we have quoted, a 'freshness' in the world. But this freshness does not accomplish its ends by hitting us over the head and compelling us ; it works by enticement and lure, by invitation and solicitation, by its own intrinsic worth and the appeal which this exercises, this calling forth a response which is freely given and therefore genuine and not 'faked'. This sort of experience, known to everybody in some degree, is for Whitehead much more a clue to the world as it goes on towards its fulfilment than would be the perhaps more obvious or blatant exercise of force which can (so to say) knock us down but never win us over.

The cosmic process, then, is characterized for Whiteheadian thought by change, dynamism, inter-relationships or organic inter-penetration, the presence of heights and depths of 'importance', and the quality of tenderness or love. And the movement is towards the realization of goods 'in greatest measure' or 'in widest commonalty spread'. But this should not be taken to mean that there is *inevitable* progress, as if one were on an escalator which willy-nilly brought one to higher levels of actualization. There are drags, back-waters, the choice of less than the fullest possible goods. In a world marked by genuine freedom, where the actual entities or occasions are themselves creative and where they may or may not elect to seek in all available ways their fulfilment or the satisfaction of their subjective aims, refusing to make their own the initial aim provided for them by God, it is highly probable, indeed nearly inevitable, that there will be failure and loss. Whitehead not only allows for this ; he recognizes it as a given fact. For him process does not mean progress in any cheap and easy sense.

On the other hand, there *is* progress, in the only significant meaning that word can have in a realistic view of things. Which is to say, there is a movement in which the chief (not the only) creative principle is able to turn that which is less than perfect or appropriate towards a good which may be realized. Thus while evil is evil and not 'partial good', God can employ it for the securing of ends which might otherwise not be within his reach. Yet one should not conclude that evil is to be done, so that good may be achieved. This would be both blasphemous and absurd. Furthermore, since God can only prehend evil in a negative way, that which is a 'surd' (as being evil) may be rejected, even while the good which may be made out of it will be accomplished. We know in our own experience that this sort of double-effect is often found ; a mistake can lead us to deeper inquiry and discovery of truth. One need only generalize from this aspect of common life to see that the same sort of thing, although not always in the same sort of way, can be affirmed of the creative process as a whole. Thus there is an ultimate optimism, in that God's faithfulness and inexhaustibility are the most effective factors in the total situation ; while at the same time there is, if not a pessimism, certainly a realism, in the appraisal of any given moment as it contributes, or fails to contribute, to the ongoing aim of good which is basic to the entire process.

In periods of world disorder, such as our own seems often to be, this may be difficult to see and accept. Yet it is no irrational or absurd attitude on man's part, when he feels somehow that there is what Schubert Ogden, following a Whiteheadian line although using his own phrases, speaks of as the abiding sense of the 'significance of life' and the worthwhile quality of existence—something that even the professed atheist seems to recognize, despite his explicit denials, since he continues to accept life and rejects the alternative choice which would be his self-destruction or suicide in the face of the evil which is present in the world. Ultimately God can be trusted to make the best of everything, even though he and the world must suffer in that making.

The Nature of Man

Whitehead never wrote a book or essay dealing with man, if by this we mean something devoted entirely and exclusively to a consideration of this topic. On the other hand, scattered through his writings there is a great deal of material which has to do with the subject—and the last section of *Adventures of Ideas* contains especially interesting paragraphs about human experience, human nature, and above all what it 'feels like to be a man' (as we might style it). Furthermore, all Whiteheadian students are indebted to Ruth Nanda Ashen for collecting these references, as well as other material, in a small volume which she has entitled *Alfred North Whitehead : His Reflections on Man and*

Nature (1961). The title itself indicates clearly the point made earlier in this chapter—Whitehead's refusal to permit any 'bifurcation' between man and the natural order in which he appears, while at the same time recognizing the distinction of 'level' and the particular quality of the human subject.

Teilhard de Chardin has spoken of what he styles 'the outside' and 'the inside' of things. Something of the same sort of distinction has often been in the present writer's mind as he reads the existentialist writers of our own day, with their careful analysis of 'human existence', and then turns back to Whitehead's metaphysical writing. One has a renewed awareness of the way in which that writing makes place for the experience which Teilhard called 'the inside', while the metaphysical portrayal of the world and man in it provides 'the outside'. It might be said, although to many this seems paradoxical at the best and absurd at the worst, that an existentialist analysis of the human situation has much in common with the Whiteheadian portrayal of what it 'feels like' to be a human experiencing subject in genuine contact with a real world. The mutual prehension in each occasion in the world and supremely (so far as conscious apprehension of the matter is concerned) in the self-awareness of each human occasion, of *ourselves*, produces a picture not too unlike that described in, say, Heidegger.

Whitehead saw man in the world, yet 'standing out from the world' (although this is not his phrase) by virtue of his capacity for conscious awareness of himself and that world, in their rich relationship one with the other. He saw man as both an embodied creature, belonging to the level of nature in its common signification but also possessing the ability to think about—to symbolize—as well as to feel that which is not himself ; he saw man's ability to engage in introspection, to think about himself and to think about himself thinking. Again, the social nature of man is very clear to Whitehead ; like every other occasion, but in a peculiarly intensive fashion, man belongs to and lives together with others—his fellow men and also everything else that plays upon him, affects him, and is affected by him. Further, man sets himself projects, for his identity is to a large degree found in the subjective aim which he, like every occasion, moves to actualize ; and in man this aim can be chosen consciously and with awareness of its implications. Finally, for Whitehead man moves towards death, since he (like all other events of which the world is made up) must 'perish'. Yet out of that 'perishing' newness can and does come—this last a point which, unlike the others so far noted, does not find a place in the usual existentialist analysis.

In the Whiteheadian view, man is a 'becoming'. He cannot be described in static terms ; he is no substance, conceived after the manner of some 'thing'. He is a living process. As such he possesses memory, which is to say that he brings together all that has gone to make him up, all that has contributed to his emergence. He is always in relationship, not only with other men but with the totality of the created order, history and nature both playing their part here. And he has his aim, his projective movement (almost, one might say in Sartrian terms his *pour-soi* to save him from sheer mass-man or *en-soi*). In the poet's words, 'man never *is* but wholly hopes *to be*'.

While Whitehead did not speak much about the question of personality, the qualities which he finds in man are such that it is proper (as Professor John Cobb has argued) to make an extension of Whiteheadian thought to secure this personal way of speaking of human nature. After all, there is rationality, there is deep feeling, there is the capacity to be in a communicating relationship with others and with the world, there is ability to receive as well as to give in such relationships, and there is genuine freedom for decision-making which enables him to strive towards his aim, rejecting that which does not seem to contribute to it or (alternatively) to 'cut off' by decision valuable possibilities and so fail to accomplish the realization of his aim in the achievement of enduring good. Hence what religious men call 'sin'. And in his 'routing' man has his own identity.

From the religious point of view, it is important to notice that Whitehead puts strong emphasis on that particular sort of human experience which feels the reality of the sacred. This experience, at first very primitive and often frightening, is rationalized as man develops through the history of the race ; it is also moralized, so that in the higher religions sheer power is no longer attributed to God but instead 'tenderness' or love becomes the dominant characteristic of deity. In *Religion in the Making* there is a detailed and faithful reporting of this experience, with its many facets, as well as an analysis of its metaphysical implications—implications which Whitehead feels fit in very well with his general position. The God known in religion is the concrete reality of God, God in his 'consequent nature' as affected by what happens in the world—the abstract concept of deity, required for explanation of the cosmos, is not *as such* experienced. God in this aspect, in his 'primordial nature', is more a requirement of metaphysics for there to be a world at all, than the 'living God' known to man. Yet that is surely the right line to take ; for in the moment of religious apprehension—in worship, say—it is no abstract deity who engages the devotion of the person thus engaged, but the vividly felt deity who is in most intimate relationship with the one who worships. Furthermore, as we have already seen and shall consider again in the next section, this deity is affected by his creatures as well as affective, and effective, in respect to them.

The long treatment of 'civilization' in *Adventures of Ideas* is also useful to us in grasping Whitehead's view of man. Through the process of growing together in community man 'comes of age' (Bonhoeffer's phrase is appropriate here). The participatory quality of human existence is central ; the past, as it is remembered and re-lived, plays its part too. This perhaps is why Whitehead is so concerned for the kind of education which will give men the sense of belonging to a growing cultural movement in which they share together in what the past has made them and move on into the future in the spirit of adventure, with 'zest' seeking for a harmony in which they can find satisfaction and fulfilment. Yet this is said without Whitehead's dismissing for a moment the role of the particular persons who are part of the community which establishes civilizations. There is a remarkable balance in his portrayal, saving it from rank individualism on the one hand and from sheer collectivism on the other.

While 'power' or 'coercion' is not ruled out altogether in Whitehead's picture of the universe, it is persuasion which is basic. We might—indeed we must—say that love is the major motif in Whitehead's view of things. This is as much true of man as of anything else. Hence Whitehead has little use for moralism. He recognizes the importance of ethics, to be sure, but for him the 'aesthetic' (in the profound sense he intends) is more important. If God is no 'ruthless moralist', man is to be 'lured', not driven, to fulfilment. It is the point of Jesus' teaching, he feels, that sympathy, kindness, love, in general a compassionate attitude, work better and are truer than anything else in respect of man's life and its meaning, just because this is how the process 'goes' at its deepest levels.

Finally, in what sense, if any, may one speak in Whitehead's terms about 'immortality' or 'life-beyond-death' for man? This question cannot properly be answered until the doctrine of God is considered, since there is no evidence (in Whitehead's thinking) for some supposedly 'natural immortality' such as Socrates could predicate of man. The reason for the denial of 'immortality' at *this* point is simply that the notion of 'soul' as a substance separable from embodiedness can find no place in the process view which Whitehead has put forward. Hence the Socratic argument is deprived of its major premiss.

In another sense, however, there *is* 'immortality'. Whitehead's Ingersoll Lecture, simply entitled 'Immortality' and included in *Essays in Science and Philosophy*, argues that all actual entities—all occurrences or occasions or events—have both factuality and value. In the former they inevitably perish as they achieve their ultimate satisfaction or completion ; in the latter they enter into, or in a better phrasing they are taken by God into his 'consequent nature' and forever are known to him, treasured by him, and employed by him in his further agency in the world to bring about increasing possibilities of good and increasing actualization of these possibilities. In that sense, at least, 'immortality' is real. This he calls 'objective immortality'. Whether or not there is some persistence of the conscious self, as a self-aware and specific routing of occasions which had both factuality and value, is another matter. Interpreters of Whitehead have differed here ; so have Christian theologians who have followed Whitehead's line of thought. For example, Schubert Ogden in *The Reality of God* (1967) seems to answer negatively ; John B. Cobb in *A Christian Natural Theology* (1965) seems to answer positively. In any event, what the *Christian* thinker will say here will be drawn not only from Whiteheadian philosophy but also from the way in which that thinker interprets the Christian revelation and its essential affirmations.

Robert Southwell once wrote some beautiful words, 'Not where I breathe, but where I love, I live'. Perhaps those words might properly be said to sum up what Whitehead has to tell us about the meaning of human nature and the nature of man.

God in Relationship

We began an earlier section of this chapter with a brief quotation from Professor Charles Hartshorne's essay on 'process-thought' as a possible 'resource' for Christian thought. Some sentences from the same essay[14] will provide an introduction to Whitehead's conception of God—God in relationship, for concretely and in fullest actuality that is the only God about whom Whitehead can speak and the only God about whom in his considered judgment anybody is able truly to speak. God utterly without relationships is for Whitehead not God at all, but an idol or a figment of men's minds.

'Perhaps immutable being is but the ultimate product of abstracting from all novelty'. Thus Hartshorne. And again : 'God is (indeed) spectator of all existence, but a sympathetic spectator who in some real sense shares in the sufferings he

14 Hartshorne, *op. cit.*, p. 47.

beholds. He is neither simply neutral to these sufferings nor does he sadistically will them for beings outside himself. He takes them into his own life and derives whatever value possible from them, but without ever wanting them to occur'.[15] What Hartshorne here says about suffering is also to be said about joy, excepting that God *does* want joy to occur. But in everything which happens God is precisely that unsurpassable 'one' who is so related to the world that it matters to him, affects him, provides new opportunities for him, and enables him to surpass *himself* (in his previous 'states') in self-expression and joy. On the other hand, nothing not-God can ever surpass him. He is the divine 'personality' who is participant in this world, who is ever to be worshipped, and who ceaselessly works to bring the greatest good out of all that occurs. Hence he is sheer *love*, and that is his 'root-attribute', if one wishes to use a traditional term.

For Whitehead God is always to be seen in the context of the cosmic process, as we showed in the earlier sections of this chapter. Since he is 'not to be treated as an exception to all metaphysical principles, invoked to save their collapse', but is 'their chief exemplification',[16] we can say of him that he too is dynamic, moving, in richest relationships with all that is not himself, more active in this place than in that (in the sense that there is an 'intensity' in the mutual awareness and in the exemplification of prehension, revealing what is always going on), and in his essential nature persuasive and loving. Furthermore, he is eminently temporal ; his 'godness' does not deny or negate time-sequence for he was active in the past, he is operative in the present, and he aims towards the future. So 'time is taken seriously', in a phrase used first (I believe) but in a different connection by Professor Leonard Hodgson. Time is *real*, not fictitious or fanciful ; and it is real for and in God as well as for and in the creation.

Whitehead's famous statement about God as no 'exception' must be rightly understood. It does not mean that God is to be

15 Hartshorne, *op. cit.*, p. 65.
16 *Process and Reality*, p. 521.

'treated' as only *another* exemplification of 'all metaphysical principles'; he is their *chief* exemplification. And in one sense, indeed, he *is* an 'exception'. He and only he persists *through all process* as the chief but not the only principle of explanation of why some particular possibilities rather than others have been, are being, or will be realized. He selects some to be realized, out of the whole infinite range of possibilities which Whitehead called in Platonic fashion 'the ideal objects': *cf.* the *Timaeus* with its 'ideal forms'. Yet this 'exception', as far as God is concerned, is not intended to remove him from being also 'in process' and required to explain the cosmos in process. Professor Donald Sherburne has lately written an essay attempting to show that the concept of God is not necessary to the Whiteheadian position; but most commentators would disagree vehemently, insisting (I think correctly) that without the concept of God the whole system falls into ruins.

For Whitehead, God is the perfect 'actual entity'. But in technical process terms, it might be better to say (with Hartshorne) that he is the 'serially-ordered routing of actual entities' which establishes him as self-identical. His nature is expressed in his agency in creation. Whatever we learn, therefore, about the principles required to understand that creation apply (although in an 'eminent manner', as scholastic analogy-doctrine would say) to deity. God is not the sheer contradiction of the world.

Thus relationship characterizes deity. God's perfection is not that of abstract being but is to be found in his capacity for, and actualization of, his relationships with that which is not himself. Hence the model for God is not some self-contained being who requires nothing for his self-existence save his own identity. The model is a richly related being whose innermost nature or quality is in his ceaseless participation and sharing. Hence, since love is relationship, sharing, being affected by, and caring, God essentially is Love.

Yet in and through his relationships he always remains God. He is supreme, unsurpassable by all not himself, and worshipful.

He may, indeed must, surpass his *present* 'state', as we might phrase it, but only by fuller realization of himself in terms of the possibilities which the creation, in its own freedom of decision, may offer him. The divine self-identity is shown by his exemplification in an eminent fashion of that which constitutes *all* self-identity—namely, faithfulness or self-consistency ; awareness and use of the past as it has happened ; capacity for relating himself without any loss ; inexhaustibility of the possession of reserves of 'strength' in love ; and purpose or subjective aim—and all this with such continuing 'enrichment' as his varying but unceasing relationships make available to him.

Thus God is 'bi-polar', to use a word suggested by Professor Hartshorne. He is *both* eternally faithful, loving, and perfect in relationships, and *also* (more concretely and 'actually') ever-lastingly (*viz.*, throughout all time) active in these ways in the given occasions. The priority, however, is not with the former and more abstract 'aspect' but with the concrete instances of his activity. These constitute him for what he is known in the world to be. Furthermore, the distinction between 'abstract' and 'concrete', or 'primorial' and 'consequent' (as Whitehead phrased it), is *only* for the purpose of analysis and discussion. The *real* God—by which is meant God as he is actually known—is the concrete, active, dynamic reality who does this or that ; and what must be said of him in more abstract terms is not the best clue to his character. For example, God acts persuasively in this or that instance, luring his creatures to the fulfilment of the initial aim that he has offered them. Thus we may say that he is faithful, persuasive, loving. But what is really meant is that he faithfully relates himself to, persuasively works within, and is lovingly affected by what goes on in the world. The verbs describing his activity are crucial ; while the verb '*is*' cannot be used in Whitehead's thought, or in that of any process-thinker, as if it were itself a substantive implying *being in an abstract sense* as the basic truth about deity.

Whitehead does not speak unequivocally about 'personality' in God—largely because he fears the distorting influence of the

D

anthropomorphic and limited human conception of 'person' which has dogged much western philosophical theology and much popular religion. Yet he explicitly attributes to God such qualities as awareness and self-awareness, the capacity to relate himself and communicate with others, the capacity also to be influenced and affected by others, freedom of choice or decision within the limits of a consistent pattern, and an intention or purpose which is his own divine 'subjective aim'. One must say, therefore, that God is understood as 'personal' in this sense, which we may think the proper sense of that word.

God's use of 'creativity'—or his love which is creative—has a central place. But creative love, or the loving moulding of creation, cannot be abstract ; to be a creator means to create, just as to be loving means to have occasions in which that love is expressed. Hence *a* creation, although of course not necess-arily this one of our present experience, seems required. To alter slightly Temple's famous statement, any world without God would not be the world about which we can meaningfully speak ; while God without some world (and for the Christian that means the sort of world about which the biblical witness informs us) would not be God in the only sense in which we can speak at all. That there should be *a* world is not optional to God, if he is creator and creative love. *What sort of world* there will be depends upon (a) ever-present creativity, (b) the decisions which God *and* the occasions in that world make and have made pos-sible, and (c) the nature of God as persuasive love who educes from this world the response which moves it towards greater sharing in his love (despite set-backs, blind alleys, and wrong choices) and hence towards the fuller realization of his purpose—a purpose which is the greatest possible participation of every-thing in that love.

How does God 'act' in the world? He acts by providing the 'lure' which evokes self-decisions in respect to his purpose of love. The decisions may be negative ; hence *lacrimae rerum*. Yet God is a creative artist, rather than a mechanical artificer or a domineering tyrant. He gives each entity its initial aim for self-realization but he does not coerce that entity to fulfil that aim. He provides occasions and opportunities for its self-realization as a 'co-creator' or, if it so chooses, for its own failure in this respect. Yet he sees to it that 'nothing is lost' which can be saved, which can contribute to the largest possible measure of realization both for him and for the other entities in the world. His action is not intrusive, as if it were from 'outside'; God is *there*, 'in the world or nowhere', working by enabling things to make themselves. None the less, this is God's world and God's work, since without him there would be neither the world as it is nor the possibilities which he makes present for it to become.

There are obvious differences, even contradictions, between 'classical theism' and a 'process theism' such as Whitehead's. We may close this section by listing some of them: (1) aseity (self-contained existence) *as contrasted with* love-in-relationship, as the root attribute of God; (2) 'being' as inclusive of becoming *as contrasted with* 'becoming' as the more inclusive term; (3) transcendence as 'unconditionedness' *as contrasted with* transcendence as perfection in love and hence relational with faithfulness to purpose or aim and an inexhaustible capacity to bring love to bear on all situations; (4) the possibility of speaking about deity in abstraction from the world *as contrasted with* the necessity for thinking of God always in terms derived from and relative to his creative activity in the world. For those who agree with Whitehead, the second alternative in each case is philosophically the more sound—and, if they are Christian theologians, biblically the only possible—choice.

A final word may be said about 'immortality', to which brief reference was made in the preceding section. 'To God only belongs immortality': this New Testament phrase may be taken to describe Whitehead's position. God persists in as well as through all process, receiving into his 'consequent' nature all that is assimilable whether by positive or negative grasp or prehension. But this means that a *kind* of immortality is bestowed on all that is thus received into God. Whitehead calls this 'objective immortality'. He would appear to have been ambiguous about what we might style 'the individual's survival of the death of the body'. Professor Hartshorne, Whitehead's distinguished contemporary expositor, rejects survival of persons after death. Yet there is nothing *in the system* to make belief in this incredible as an 'act of faith' based on other evidence— say, the resurrection of Christ. This is a matter with which the Christian theologian must wrestle. On the other hand, it is certainly plain that *any* teaching about 'survival' which can claim to be genuinely religious and truly Christian must predicate of God unfailing love for and care of his creatures. In that sense, at least, Thornton Wilder's words in *The Bridge of San Luis Rey* are true for both process-thought and for Christian faith, 'Love is the only survival, the only meaning'.

Attitude to Christian Faith

We have already noted Whitehead's sympathetic attitude towards religion and religious experience. He insisted that the 'fact of the religious vision' is an abidingly important element in human life. In any philosophy which hopes to be adequate to all the facts, he said, that vision must be regarded very seriously. Whitehead was not a religious apologist; his books were not written specifically to make a case for the vision about whose importance he was convinced. Neither was he a theologian, concerned with developing the Christian implications of his thought. He was a scientist who had become a philosopher— and what he says must always be understood in that way, with due regard to his own interpretation of the meaning and the purpose of philosophy.

In Whitehead's view, religion is 'the art and theory of the internal life of man, so far as it depends on the man himself, and on what is permanent in the nature of things'.[17] The book from which this quotation is made should be read carefully by any who wish to see how Whitehead worked out the way in which

[17] *Religion in the Making*, p. 58.

this definition is demonstrated in the history of religion and in the practice of religion by contemporary man. If the book is read as a whole, it will be apparent that there has been great mis-understanding of a famous sentence in it : 'Religion is what the individual does with his solitariness', and of the related com-ment, 'If you are never solitary, you are never religious'.[18] Whitehead did *not* mean that the religious man is by definition a 'solitary'. He *did* mean, as the context of these two sentences shows, that if religion is vital and 'real' it must be apprehended in the inner place of each man's personal life. Religion which does not bring a man starkly up against 'the nature of things'— and this must happen to each man for himself—is simply con-ventional or 'customary'. It 'cuts no ice' with a man unless it is his own.

On the other hand, Whitehead insisted on the social nature of religion, which expresses itself in beliefs or 'myths' (as he put it) and in 'ritual' with its accompanying 'emotion'. In all 'inferior' religions, the stress on 'ritual' and 'myth' and the accompanying 'emotion' is not rationalized and moralized. Yet such religion is not to be despised. It is an inevitable moment in the develop-ment of the full religious vision. When in the course of his becoming 'civilized' man realizes the necessity of, and the place for, his own personal assent and participation, religion becomes deeply internal—although the social expression of it, as of all human concerns, can never be minimized or forgotten.

The danger to religion in its earlier phase, when it is *merely* 'social', is that it will lack depth and become the careless and thoughtless following of the customs of the group. When this danger comes to be understood, the great prophets appear speaking of the importance of that personal (or individual) apprehension which redeems the enterprise from its tendency to shallowness and conventionality. So it now becomes social in a new sense ; it is conscious and conscientious participation in the shared experiences of men as they seek to grasp and be grasped by the nature of things at its deepest level—that is, by God himself.

[18] *Religion in the Making*, pp. 58 and 17.

It is not necessary for us to pursue the subject here. *Religion in the Making* is an eminently readable book, remarkable for its insight and sprinkled with aphoristic comments which with deep penetration make points that force the reader to think deeply about his own understanding of whatever religious conviction and experience he may possess. What is of interest to us is Whitehead's attitude towards the particular religion in which he was brought up—not Anglicanism, of course, but Christianity itself.

This discussion is found in parts of the book already mentioned, but it is developed most interestingly in the chapter on 'The New Reformation' in *Adventures of Ideas*. Often he speaks sharply about certain aspects in the Christian tradition—for example, he has much to say negatively about the Old Testament stress in that tradition, a matter which also comes up for comment in his reported conversations. He admired the Jewish prophets for their moral courage but he regarded as unfortunate their idea of God as 'a' person who directly controls his world ; he also disliked the 'ruthless moral ruler' whom (as he thought) they proclaim, for while he recognized the inevitable moral development of the 'idea of God' he felt that such a picture must be inhuman and 'un-divine'. Nor did he hesitate to express his distaste for the last book of the New Testament, the *Revelation of St John the Divine*, which he regarded as barbaric in mood and untouched by the spirit of Jesus.

On the other hand, his reverence for Jesus was unlimited.

The life of Christ is not an exhibition of over-ruling power. Its glory is for those who can discern it, and not for the world. Its power lies in its absence of force. It has the decisiveness of a supreme ideal, and that is why the history of the world divides at this point of time.[19]

For him Jesus is 'the revelation in act' of the structured dynamic which is most profound in the nature of things ; Jesus in the totality of his life discloses 'the nature of God' and 'God's agency in the world'. The God disclosed in Jesus is no inert absolute, neither is he an oriental sultan demanding servile

[19] *Religion in the Making*, p. 57.

obedience ; he is not ruthless in his moral demands, nor is he so transcendent that he has little if any contact with the world and with men. On the contrary, he is sheer persuasion or love-in-act. It is the tragedy of the Christian Church, Whitehead said, that it has failed to keep this vision of God seen in Jesus, and this understanding of God's way of acting in the world, consistently and faithfully in the central place. It has even been prepared, he thought, to 'attribute to God that which belongs exclusively to Caesar'.

For much Christian theology Whitehead had great respect. He believed that the early Church Fathers in particular, and especially the Alexandrine apologists, had discerned the problem which is posed to philosophy by the fact of Christ's life. This is the question how God is related to his world, how God can be transcendent to the events in which he is immanently at work, and how he can be thus immanent without losing the qualities which make him divine. The *Logos* doctrine of the Patristic Age appealed to him, for it dealt faithfully with this question. In *Adventures of Ideas* he commended the *Logos* doctrine ; but it is equally clear that he felt that to confine 'incarnation' (a term which he wished to use for all divine activity in the world) to Jesus alone is to him a mistake. He wished to see Jesus as the representative and even the decisive 'incarnation' of God, which in degree but certainly not in kind is to be distinguished from other instances of 'divine agency'.

Whitehead was not opposed to 'dogma', in the sense of statements drawn up to express the significance of facts known in faith ; but he was convinced that dogma must not be 'fixed', so that change would seem blasphemous to believers. Perhaps his choice of words in this respect was not fortunate ; had he been a professional theologian he might have made a distinction between 'dogma' as a minimal statement of Christian conviction in respect to God and God's working in the world (supremely in Jesus Christ), and those speculative theological opinions which as a matter of history and observation we know to have changed from time to time. But his point is sound, at any rate, in so far as he desired that there should be an openness and a generosity of spirit among theologians, with a willingness to modify their opinions if and when this should be required.

The sense in which Whitehead may himself be called a Christian will engage our attention in the final chapter. But we can say that he was not only a 'religious man' but also one who (perhaps as the result of his early life and training) had a definitely Christian attitude towards the world and his fellow-men. He might be described as 'detached' so far as much conventional Christianity in his own day was concerned ; at the same time he was also plainly 'attached', in that for him the 'Galilean vision' was at the heart of his thinking about religion. Even more, it was at the heart of his own vision of the world, of man, and of the divine persuasion which he firmly believed was the truth most profoundly and deeply given to men. He might well have said that the master-light of all his seeing, illuminating for him the entire range of experience in its widest sense, was to be found in the Johannine verse, 'God is love ; and he that abideth in love abideth in God and God in him'.

3

Significance

Christian Process-Theology

IN an essay published a few years ago, Professor H. H. Price spoke of theism as 'a metaphysics of love'. One may question whether every theistic system has in fact been such a metaphysics. Indeed it might be said, with Professor Hartshorne, that much 'classical theism'—the variety which is most familiar to us—has so stressed God's independence, aseity and absoluteness, his character as 'un-moved mover', first cause, or 'ground of being', that love hardly seems to be his essential quality or characteristic. After all, love cannot be known save in relationships, in being affected as well as affecting, in sharing and participation.

It is that aspect which is strongly stressed in process-thinking; Whitehead was insistent that the concrete actuality of God is found there, rather than in the more abstract aspects of the divine nature. In his own idiom, the God who is in fact encountered by us is God in his 'consequent nature', not in his 'primordial nature'. And, as we have seen, God in his consequent aspect is persuasive, sympathetic, affected by all that is not himself, inclusive of all possible good, supremely tender—indeed, God so portrayed is Love. Perhaps better, he is the cosmic Lover who tenderly, luringly, persuasively, faithfully, indefatigably, inexhaustibly (for he never comes to the end of his caring) relates himself to, cares for, and brings all possible good out of, the world.

Hence we may say that process-metaphysics is indeed 'a metaphysics of love'. That is one of the chief reasons that it has seemed to many contemporary Christian theologians to provide a

E

conceptuality for Christian faith and a context within which Christian theology may be 'done'. However, this is not the only reason for the appeal which it has had. Obviously the primary reason is that these thinkers are convinced that it is true, as true a vision of 'how things go' as we are likely to get, even when it is granted that it cannot claim finality any more than any other philosophy. It is our best insight into 'reality'. Furthermore, those who work with this philosophy believe that it fits in with what we have come to know about the world from scientific enquiry, both at the physical level and in biological, sociological, and psychological study. Finally, they think that it can make sense of the 'aesthetic' quality in experience and in the world— the 'feeling-tones' which accompany our awareness of things as well as of persons, the valuational and appreciative side of life as we know it in our most sensitive moments. Whitehead's vision—however difficult may be his manner of expressing it in words—speaks to them as veridical ; and that in a fashion which, as they judge, is not equalled by other accounts of 'process and reality'.

Among these Christian thinkers today, there are several seniors and many juniors. The older men include American theologians like Barnard E. Meland, for many years Professor of Constructive Theology at the University of Chicago, Professor Daniel Day Williams, Professor of Theology at Union Seminary in New York City, and Professor Bernard Loomer, Professor at the Graduate Theological Union in Berkeley, California. All these are well over fifty years of age. The younger American theologians are too numerous to list, but two who have written extensively are Professor Schubert Ogden of the Perkins School of Theology in Dallas, Texas, and Professor John Cobb of the School of Theology at Claremont, California. In the British Isles, the name of Peter N. Hamilton, whose recent book *The Living God and the Modern World* is notably clear and incisive, may stand for several others now at work in producing an English version of 'process-theology'.

We have said that Whitehead was not a theologian. He was a

mathematician and philosopher of science who in the last quarter of his life turned to the more general issues of metaphysics. So also with Hartshorne, the distinguished contemporary expositor of Whitehead who has done so much to develop 'process-philosophy'. Hartshorne is professionally a philosopher—and a distinguished ornithologist—and theological concerns are secondary to his main interest. Because of this background in strict philosophy, 'process-thought' must be worked through, not simply 'taken over', by Christian theologians. In a way not dissimilar to that of Augustine with his use of neo-Platonism, or of Thomas Aquinas with his similar use of the newly recovered Aristotelianism of his day, the exponents of 'process-theology' have found in Whitehead's vision of the world material which in their judgment provides a context for Christian faith and a conceptuality with which Christian theologians can work. But it must be adapted to the purpose.

For example, to take one instance crucial for Christian theology, there is no discussion of christology and soteriology in the writings of Whitehead. These are not the concern of a philosopher as such. On the other hand, there is in Whitehead an insistence on the mutual prehensions of God and man, a concept of disclosure (through event or occurrence) of what is going on in the world, and a recognition that certain moments or points can and do have 'importance' for our understanding. What Whitehead says about these can be useful to the Christian thinker as he seeks to give expression to the abiding Christian experience that Jesus Christ, a man in history, is in a special sense 'the act of God' in human life. So also Whitehead's constant emphasis on the centrality of love, both in human affairs and in the cosmic process, his references to the compassion of God and the self-identification of God with the world, and his insistence on organic or societal affects, provide material in terms of which the Christian thinker may begin his interpretation of what Christian experience asserts about 'the saving work' of Jesus Christ. The specifically Christian data supply material which can provide for a further development and also a correction of 'process-thought'. Not only does the Christian faith go beyond what this conceptuality has to say ; it also makes necessary some important modifications in it.

None the less, Whitehead's stress on God as being not 'the exception to metaphysical principles, to save them from collapse, but their chief exemplification', is taken with great seriousness by the theologians we are discussing. It is precisely because the world is processive, dynamic, societal or organismic, the sphere of novel emergents or occasions with particular moments of high significance, that God may be seen as living, related, active, and disclosed particularly in certain 'high' moments. It is because persuasion is characteristic of the world that 'the divine who is to be worshipped' can without absurdity be interpreted in the light of the specific Christian event as indeed Love—and this without succumbing to the stark irrationality which would assert the divine Love in spite of everything else that man might think. There is a certain 'fit' here between 'process-philosophy' and Christian faith.

Nor is this relationship to be explained away by saying that Whitehead and his expositors are the products of a Christian culture and hence it is to be expected that their thought will be coloured by Christian ideas. The truth is that every system of thought is influenced by the cultural context in which it appears, just as the thinking of any man is affected by his environment and his heredity. Yet this fact does not mean that a man's thinking can never be adequate to the facts, nor that a given philosophical vision is totally vitiated by its cultural grounding. The question in each instance is not whether such influence has occurred ; of course it has, or there could be no human thinking at all. The real question is whether the thinking stands up under criticism ; whether it provides a coherent account of the facts which may be validated, in some fashion or other, by its logical consistency and by its capacity to account for the data which experience provides. The situation is not unlike that of the man charged by the psychologist with rationalization. Professor Leonard Hodgson once remarked in the face of such a charge that the reply is, 'Yes, this may be rationalization. The question is not whether that is the case, for I may say the same thing to you on your own terms—all your criticism is also rationalization. *Tu quoque*. But that is not the question. The question is, does my thinking, does your thinking, exhibit loyalty to the given data, survive trenchant criticism, and make sense in the light of the rest of what we think we know?'

It may be—indeed I believe it is the case—that Whitehead's vision of the world and of God in relation to the world could only have appeared in a cultural milieu such as the history of Christian civilization provides. But the same is true, as Whitehead and others have demonstrated, in respect to that particular kind of science which we in the west believe to be of such enormous importance in helping us understand our world. The Jewish emphasis on particular events, the doctrine of creation in which the world is seen as open to investigation precisely because it is not in itself divine, and Greek rationalism with its logic and its boldness in seeking the facts, were united in Christian culture to make such science possible. No Christian theologian need be troubled by the fact that 'process-philosophy' appeared within the stream of history which we call Christian.

The Christians who use 'process-thought' accept the doctrine that God cannot be utterly contradictory to the world in which his activity is carried on. They believe that God himself is 'in process', in the sense that he is not abstractly eternal, utterly above and beyond all temporal succession. Rather, they see him as eminently temporal, although the divine 'time' is different from, yet not the denial of, the temporality experienced in the world. Again, they believe that God fulfils himself, not by some imposed necessity but by his own nature as creative love, through taking into his life what goes on in the creation. He is indeed unsurpassable by anything other than himself ; that is the definition of his divinity. Yet he is able to surpass himself, so far as his 'experience' goes. He is enriched in his opportunities and occasions for self-expression in the world as that world with its genuine freedom responds or fails to respond to him and as he himself employs for good all the opportunities and occasions which are available to him.

Above all, God is seen not as primarily the 'unmoved mover' or 'first cause' or 'absolute reality' but as the supremely related one. His relationship with creation is not simply logical on his side even if contingent on the world's side; it is active and living, involving him in a creation which matters to him to such a degree that he is not only causative in it but affected by it. He works by his persuasion, through his lure or attraction or appeal, not by the exercise of arbitrary power. So the words used of God in a familiar hymn are correct : 'Pure universal Love thou art'.

The several points noted in the last chapter in respect to White-head's view of the world are felt by process-theologians to have a remarkably apt relation to the symbols in biblical thought. Those biblical symbols can be taken with the utmost seriousness, although not with a wooden literalism. We may summarize the position in this fashion.

History and nature are moving towards a goal which is God's sovereign rule; and God is involved in them, guiding and luring them towards that goal. He is the living God, who works in his creation tirelessly yet inexhaustibly to bring about the realization of the potentialities which he has implanted there. He provides both the 'initial aim' and the final goal; at every point he is actively engaged in persuading the creation to accept that aim for its own and to move towards that goal as its fulfilment. As the living God he has a purpose for his world and he is 'in the world' to effect that purpose—not by arbitrary imposition or interference but by eliciting the 'amen' of the creatures to the enormous good he offers them. This good is the actualization of their potentiality as well as God's achievement of his purpose.

In the creative process he has permitted radical freedom, so that evil is a possibility, and among men sinful decision can (and does) lead to tragic situations. Yet God's love is faithful and inexhaustible; it is able to 'take' this evil and sin, to absorb what is bad and to use what is good. In spite of evil and sin, good can emerge through the patient, tender, never-failing 'over-ruling' of God as he provides for and 'governs' his world in love. It is incorrect to say, as some critics have done, that 'process-theology' does not take with sufficient seriousness the facts of evil and sin. Whitehead could never be accused of this, nor for that matter could Teilhard de Chardin, who is often and rightly classified as a 'process-thinker'. Of course the way in which evil and sin are understood by these thinkers departs from the conventional view ; but the fact is not in question. Nor is it in question for the theologians who follow this line.

In the world there are places or points which have what Whitehead called 'importance'. In this or that occasion, there is a particularly intense and vivid concentration of creative act and response ; this may be taken as providing a clue or key to the purpose running through the whole process. In Scripture, the history of the Jewish people is seen as 'important' ; and for all Christians the event of Jesus Christ is regarded as supremely 'important'. In Christ's life, where divine initiating activity is met by human response at its highest, God is seen for what he is and for what he is always doing. Hence, in a phrase which the present writer has often found helpful, Jesus is not to be taken as the supreme anomaly, making nonsense of other events that have happened, are happening, or will happen ; he is the classical instance, disclosing in act what God is 'up to' in his creation— and at the same time, because of the adequacy of his human response to God's initiative, expressing what man may become. Nor is this merely demonstration ; it is an effective act, for the intensification is 'objective' since God is involved, as well as 'subjective' since human response is present. The drawing of men to Christ establishes a level of life, a depth of existence, which may rightly be described, in St Paul's phrase, as 'in Christ', and hence 'in Love' (in God). This event makes an enormous difference, not only in principle but in fact. God can do now what previously and elsewhere he could not do if he respected (as he always does) the freedom of his creation to respond in answering love to his initiating act as Love.

How to state in process-terms the union of God and m

Christ has been an important concern for process theologians. Some of them would speak with Schubert Ogden of the awareness of the divine purpose by the man Jesus ; others would emphasize with John Cobb the possibility of mutual prehensions in which God grasps the totality of the human life which—through the guidance of creation and especially of man by the lure and appeal and persuasion which we have noted—was born of Mary. In the latter view, Jesus is that man who was prehended or grasped by the reality of the divine activity in the conditions of time and place in which he lived, as he himself prehended or grasped the divine activity operative there. The best analogy would be the way in which in a loving relationship two lives can be distinct yet inseparable. The famous Chalcedonian adverbs might apply in a special sense ; we have a union of God and man that is truly personal, yet in which God and man are brought into unity unconfusedly, unchangeably (in at least some senses), inseparably, and indivisibly. When two human beings love one another in the most profound way, there is a unity which is entirely moral and personal, and yet is real and abiding. The interpenetration of lives in love establishes union in its most intimate personal sense.

Thus we can say that God acts here, as he acts always, in love. He is love, not a cosmic tyrant who demands servile obeisance or the 'big boss with the "big stick" ' ; neither is he 'the ruthless moral ruler' who requires men 'to be good' before he will accept them. He is 'pure unbounded love' in his own nature and in his action in the creation. He is abidingly faithful, unfailing at work, inexhaustible in the resources of his love. Thus he is 'transcendent', in the only proper meaning of that word, even while he is also 'immanent', since he is (in Whitehead's words which we have already quoted) 'in the world, or nowhere, creating continually in us and around us'.

Surely this picture is not too remote from what the biblical symbols are saying, drawn as they are from human existence at given times and places and yet intended to be indicative of what is ever true of God in his dealings with his creation.

The meaning of man is also illuminated. Man is a dynamic creature, moving towards fulfilment yet free to decide against this fulfilment. He is bound together with his brethren, and indeed with the whole historical and natural order, open to their influence upon him yet entirely responsible in his decisions. He may make, or fail to make, his proper contribution to the achievement of the divine purpose. He is 'becoming', with strong desires that may be rationally known ; but his true achievement or self-realization is only as he loves. In God's intention he is such a lover, yet he is frustrated in his loving, and in consequence of wrong decisions he may and does distort that which is deepest in him. Thus he is a 'sinner ; he needs what we might style 're-alignment' with the divine intention for him. His sinning is not so much disobedience to some moral code, some set of commandments, or some imposed law ; it is a violation of his loving relationship with God and his fellows and hence a violation of his own drive towards love.

Other aspects of the Christian faith are open to similar re-conception when the insights of 'process-thought' are taken in context. From one point of view the results may seem novel, not least because love is taken seriously as the principal clue to the meaning of the entire Christian reality. Yet the results are not negative like those which follow from some other ways of re-conceiving the Christian message—certainly they are less revolutionary than the denial of metaphysics or the attempt to speak of the gospel in terms which altogether reject reference to God as central to that gospel or refuse to engage in 'God-talk' because (following the dictate of a philosophical school in our own day) such talk is thought to have no verification in scientific or quasi-scientific experiment or observation.

On this last point, we may note that 'process-philosophy' has consistently declined to accept the 'veto' on God and 'God-talk'. It has pointed to the fact that common human experience claims to have some transcendent reference ; it has insisted on the inescapable demand made by the human mind for explanation in more inclusive and adequate terms than those provided in scientific observation and experiment ; and it has appealed to the 'aesthetic'—the feeling-tones, appreciation, evaluation, and deeply 'sensed' experience—as providing valuable data for any soundly based and adequate interpretation of man and his world. Perhaps this is why so many thinkers who have recognized the insufficiency of a purely scientific approach to reality have been drawn to 'process-philosophy'—a point that is made in Professor Ian G. Barbour's magisterial volume *Issues in Science and Religion* (1967), where a natural scientist confesses the attraction of this metaphysic and finds it very helpful in his own reconstructive philosophical and theological effort.

Is such a religious and Christian use of 'process-philosophy' in accordance with Whitehead's own thinking? In attempting to answer this question, we must again recall that Whitehead was not a theologian, nor did he think and write with any specifically theological end in view. Hence it is impossible to find in his work the sort of development which has been undertaken by those who in one way or another would call themselves his Christian theological disciples. But he was a religious man, profoundly influenced by his Christian upbringing in a clerical home and greatly affected by what he believed to be the Christian contribution to philosophical wisdom. But he was not an orthodox Christian, at least in any conventional meaning of that phrase.

An acquaintance of the writer, who was a student at Harvard while Whitehead was a professor there, has told of a conversation in which he asked his teacher whether the philosophy which he was expounding could be reconciled with 'Christian orthodoxy'. Whitehead, he said, answered the question in the negative. But we must ask what Whitehead understood the question to imply. There can be no doubt that he took his questioner to mean by 'Christian orthodoxy' the rather narrow and (as he often said) incredible dogmatic structure which as a child he had been taught. Yet we have been told that in his years in Cambridge, England, Whitehead attended church with fair regularity ; it is said that he went to a so-called 'high' parish, amusing evidence for which is found in *Process and Reality*, where he mentions incense as a typical 'religious' symbol, evocative of feeling-tones which mysteriously communicate profound truth. At Cambridge, Massachusetts, he attended the nearby parish church until his later years, when he began going from time to time to the University Memorial Church. If he did not think that his philosophy was reconcilable with 'Christian orthodoxy', he certainly thought that what in *Adventure of Ideas* he called (was it the first use of the phrase?) 'the new Reformation' was bound to come and he welcomed its coming. He did not have much sympathy with the kind of 'liberal theology' which he felt reduced the assertions of the historic faith to pietistic and moralistic admonitions ; indeed he once remarked that 'the defect' of that kind of theology was that it 'confined itself to the suggestion of minor, vapid reasons why people should continue to go to church in the traditional fashion'.[20]

We end this book by quoting what has seemed to many Whitehead's most beautiful piece of writing.[21] The passage occurs at the place where Whitehead is arguing that 'the power of Christianity lies in its revelation in act, of that which Plato divined in theory'—that persuasion, not coercion, is the proper interpretation of the principle 'by reason of which ideals are effective in the world and forms of order evolve'. Here are Whitehead's words, which in my own judgment show him to have been Christian in spirit and also provide a basis for the Christian use of his philosophy :

The essence of Christianity is the appeal to the life of Christ as a revelation of the nature of God and of his agency in the world. The record is fragmentary, inconsistent, and uncertain. It is not necessary for me to express any opinion as to the proper reconstruction of the most likely tale of historic fact. Such a procedure would be useless, without value, and entirely out of place in this book. But there can be no doubt as to what elements in the record have evoked a response from all that is best in human nature. The Mother, the Child, and the bare manger : the lowly man, homeless and self-forgetful, with his message of peace, love, and sympathy : the suffering, the agony, the tender words as life ebbed, the final despair : and the whole with the authority of supreme victory.

[20] *Adventures of Ideas*, p. 174.
[21] *Ibid.*, p. 170.

A man who would write a passage like that and who could frame a philosophy which insisted on that vision as the supreme moment not only in religious history but also in the way the world is creatively ordered and guided, can hardly be denied the name Christian. Nor can the use of his thought for Christian purposes be regarded as illegitimate.

Brief Bibliography

BOOKS BY WHITEHEAD

(5 selected from 18 publications)

Science and the Modern World, 1925

Religion in the Making, 1926

Process and Reality ; An Essay in Cosmology, 1929
 (best read in conjunction with D. S. Sherburne, *A Key to
 Whitehead's Process and Reality*, 1965)

The Adventures of Ideas, 1938

Modes of Thought, 1938

 All published by Cambridge University Press.

BOOKS ABOUT WHITEHEAD'S THOUGHT

Emmet, D. M., *Whitehead's Philosophy of Organism*, Macmillan,
 1932

Johnson, A. M., *Whitehead's Theory of Reality*, Dover, 1952
                Whitehead's Philosophy of Civilization, Dover, 1958

Lowe, Victor, *Understanding Whitehead*, Johns Hopkins, 1962

Peters, F. H., *The Creative Advance*, Bethany, 1966

BOOKS ABOUT PROCESS-THEOLOGY

Hamilton, P. N., *The Living God and the Modern World*, Hodder
 & Stoughton, 1967

Hartshorne, Charles, *Man's Vision of God*, Harper, 1941

James, Ralph F., *The Concrete God*, Bobbs-Merrill, 1968

Ogden, Schubert, *The Reality of God*, S.C.M. Press, 1967

Pittenger, Norman, *Process-Thought and Christian Faith*, S.C.M.
 Press, 1968